Praise for "Chef Ricar
to Succ

I love this new book by Chef Ricardo entitled "Chef Ricardo's Secret Recipes to Success: From Poverty to Purpose." I am delighted that Chef Ricardo has written this inspirational book about his life and journey as a YouTuber.

This book will inspire many who have a dream that they want to achieve. Readers of all ages who have an interest in inspirational stories will find this book most appealing.

Kirly-Sue
Vegan Chef, Author,
YouTuber & Social Media Personality

Chef Ricardo's new book: Secret Recipes to Success, is a must-read. He is a respectful and respectable gentleman man full of honour and integrity, who is so much in touch and proud of his humble beginnings.

We all need to take a leaf out of Ricardo's beautiful book, that anything is possible and achievable if you put your mind to it.

A man with a great vision with a positive determination to succeed in every step of the way.

It is definitely inspirational and uplifting, and I recommend and vouch that this book is an absolute life changer.

Kwame Owusu
Administrator

Chef Ricardo's new book "From Poverty to Purpose" is an inspirational story depicting his journey from the small town of Ocho Rios, Jamaica to becoming a world-renowned chef with a huge social media following.

This book is a must read, demonstrating what can be achieved with hard work, purpose and dedication.

Hugo Ng
Senior Talent Manager, Studio71.

CHEF RICARDO'S SECRET

SECRET

RECIPES TO SUCCESS

Also by Chef Ricardo

Caribbean Cuisine Cookbook

FROM POVERTY TO PURPOSE

CHEF RICARDO'S SECRET

RECIPES TO SUCCESS

BambuSparks

Published by
BambuSparks Publishing
4 Rochester Avenue,
Kingston 8
Jamaica, W. I.
www.bambusparks.com

Editors: Tamara McKayle and Zoe Simpson

Layout by: BambuSparks Publishing

Cover Design: Olivia ProDesigns

Photos: Chef Ricardo

For feedback, bulk orders or speaking engagements, contact the author at ricardobook@hotmail.co.uk.

To my dear grandma Ms. Dottie,
who told me I'd become a Chef one day.
Thanks for believing in me.

PREFACE

At the start of 2023, a young lady from Jamaica invited me on her YouTube show "The Trailblazers with Tamara McKayle TV Show" to share my own story and journey to success despite the odds. I agreed. It impacted me deeply and inspired me to put pen to paper, especially from the feedback I received from those who watched the episode on YouTube.

Most of you know me as *'Chef Ricardo'* but not many know the journey and story of Ricardo 'Ricky' Campbell and how I evolved to become the man you know me as today.

All the stories shared are real-life experiences on my journey and path to date. My book is for anyone who aims to believe in themselves despite the challenges or obstacles they have faced or are facing today. No obstacle is too great for a life of blessings and opportunities that are before you. Just believe in yourself.

CONTENTS

INTRODUCTION

YOU CAN HAVE THE LIFE OF YOUR DREAMS IF YOU FOCUS LONG ENOUGH

YouTube changed my life a million percent! That's what I always tell people. From growing up poor in Jamaica to today living my dream life seemed impossible to many, but it wasn't.

When I left Jamaica and migrated to the United Kingdom years ago, I thought that success and financial freedom would come through the traditional avenues, and they did in some respects. However, it was the internet, specifically YouTube, that changed my fortunes.

Perhaps you are feeling like you are in a rut. Perhaps you are unhappy with your life as it is, and you are wanting a change. You may be desiring to earn more income, but at the same time, not sure how to achieve your purpose or vision. You may even be looking for some ideas on twinning your passion to YouTube and growing your audience. I want to tell you, my friend, it's okay. I've been there too.

While I enjoy sharing scrumptious recipes to nourish your body, I hope you will use all my secret recipes to success to become the best version of yourself. This is the reason for *Chef Ricardo's Secret Recipes to Success.* I am going to show you how to dig deep within yourself; how to focus and win at life even if the odds have been stacked against you. I'll also tap into my journey and strategies from being a poor lad in Jamaica, passionate about cooking, to now living my dream life as an award-winning Chef, cooking in front of millions daily through my YouTube platform with over 1.5 million subscribers; becoming my own boss, and gaining enough wealth to transform my life.

Each chapter is designed to make you a winner, no matter your age, background, career, or current realities. Additionally, if you're interested in making it big time in the lucrative world of YouTube, this book also offers you some insights into achieving that goal. Take it from me, as I will show you how I started from scratch with no money, connection, or what we in Jamaica call 'links', but accomplished success.

If you want a better life, this book is for you. If you want to become a success, this book is for you. If you want to become your own boss, and be in charge of your time, your hours, and your earning opportunities, this book is for you. Don't delay or procrastinate and put off that dream for another day, week, month, or worse years; we all know how time quickly passes. Be purposeful about your life. Be purposeful about your future. Be purposeful about your destiny. ACT RIGHT NOW!

If I did it after losing both parents at a young age, struggling in Jamaica to become the man that I am today, then, surely my friend, you can do it too. Happy reading!

CHAPTER 1

LOOKING BACK

I grew up in rural Jamaica, in the small community of Mount Moriah in the parish of St. Ann. When I was very young, my mom died from a debilitating illness. My father subsequently passed away when I was a teenager. He had been on the farm work programme in America for many years, and so he often travelled back and forth from America to Jamaica. Rumours say he was poisoned. He left behind three of us as brothers, and one sister. With all this happening, the main figure in my life was my maternal grandma, Miss Dottie. She raised me to become the man I am today, Chef Ricardo.

It was my grandma's cooking, and resourcefulness in the kitchen which sparked my early interest in cooking and has led me to become a successful chef with a large following on YouTube from millions of people around the world.

Life in Jamaica

Life in Jamaica wasn't easy economically, but those were fun times living with Miss Dottie in rural Jamaica, in the countryside, or as we call it in 'the bush'. Even though we were poor, I never really felt lack because I was happy. I especially enjoyed grandma making my favourite dishes; I loved participating too. In fact, a mark I have on my tummy bears witness to my early interest in, and love for cooking. I will never forget that day. Ms. Dottie was cooking in the outside kitchen which, back then, was a common occurrence for Jamaican families. The outside kitchen, as the name suggests, is a kitchen built on the outdoors separate from the main house. It was really more of a small shed. Cooking would be done using a coal stove, which used wood and coal as the fuel.

Well, one day, Grandma was cooking, and since I loved to hang around the kitchen, and being the little inquisitive fellow that I was, I got a little too close to the pot. Well, the pot fell on me, leaving me with that 'cooking mark', as I refer to it today. Immediately following the incident, Ms. Dottie, in her distinct Jamaican accent said, *'Ricky, yu gwine be a Chef one day.'* I believed her.

So, yes, I would always watch Grandma when she was cooking, and she would often go to the farm to reap various vegetables, ground provisions, and organic food to eat on a daily basis. Among the produce would be the red kidney beans to use in the preparation of red peas soup, which I thoroughly enjoyed. At Christmas time, for instance, she would reap the sorrel plant which is popular in Jamaica to make a red Christmas beverage. That, too, was a refreshing favourite.

In other instances, Grandma would purchase pork from the community butcher, and prepare and serve the family various mouth-watering meals. Wonderful memories of my time living with Grandma Dottie. She did everything for me: wash and iron my clothes, tidy my room; prepare my meals; you name it. I grew up in quite a nurturing environment. I simply cannot forget where I came from. You shouldn't either!

Although Grandma told me that one day I would become a chef, I also had to believe that. It was important for me to believe in myself. As a teenager I went in search of my dream job, visiting many hotels in Ocho Rios, St. Ann, which is a tourist-laden area on the North Coast of Jamaica. I even came close to being employed at the popular entertainment spot, Margaritaville, in the parish, but I was denied because I was too young.

After several unsuccessful applications, I finally landed an opportunity at the popular Sandcastles Hotel in Ocho Rios. Well, despite my lofty goal to be a Chef, the job I got was as a kitchen assistant, essentially to help around the kitchen, washing the dishes, and doing basic tasks like preparing vegetables. But you know what, I never complained. I did the washing while observing and learning on the job from the Chefs there.

Eventually, due to my eagerness, I was also given the opportunity to help prepare simple meals like Jamaica's national dish, ackee and salt fish, our Sunday staple, rice and peas, and other dishes like brown stew chicken.

The skills and knowledge that I acquired at the Sandcastles Hotel enabled me to gain full-time employment in the hotel industry in Jamaica which I did for several years. During that time, I worked in positions such as a Range Chef on the buffet line, at the grill on the outside, and several other positions. My duties included cooking, working as the temperature control officer, and ensuring that the presentation of the dishes was maintained to a high standard.

During this period of my life, I also enrolled in a popular skills training College on the island called HEART Trust/NSTA (Human Employment and Resource Training Trust/National Training Agency) known to most Jamaicans simply as 'HEART.' It was at that institution that I honed, and perfected my culinary skills and obtained my Chef certificate. I later earned my National Vocational Qualifications (NVQ) certification as a Chef. Looking back, it was all preparation for the next chapters of my life.

Chef Ricardo with his
certificate from HEART
TRUST/NSTA in Jamaica

Chef Ricardo in his early
years as a Chef in Jamaica.

Chef Ricardo's dearly
beloved Grandmother 'Miss
Dottie' to the left in blue.

Success Recipes from Chapter 1

My friend, life is a journey that is full of ups and downs. Those early years reminded me that every experience that we go through shapes us into the person we are today. I want you to, likewise, look at your past as a fuel for your future success. Whether our experiences are positive or negative, they can teach us valuable lessons that we can use to prepare for the future.

One of the most significant ways that past experiences prepare us for the future is by teaching us resilience. Resilience is the ability to bounce back from difficult situations. When we face challenges, we learn how to overcome them, and this builds our resilience. The more resilient we are, the better equipped we are to handle future challenges.

Another way that past experiences prepare us for the future is by teaching us problem-solving skills. When we face a problem, we have to find a solution. This requires us to think critically and identify and apply creative solutions to the problem. The more we practice problem-solving, the better we become at it. This skill is invaluable in the future, as we will, undoubtedly, face many challenges that require us to think outside the proverbial box.

Past experiences also teach us the importance of perseverance. When we face obstacles, it can be tempting to give up. However, if we persevere, we can overcome even the most challenging situations. This skill is essential in the future, as we will, undoubtedly, face setbacks and failures. If we can persevere through these challenges, we will be better equipped to achieve our goals.

Another way that past experiences prepare us for the future is by teaching us empathy. This is the ability to relate to others who are going through similar situations. Empathy allows us to be more compassion-nate and understanding towards others. Empathy also allows us to be able to offer support to others as they experience challenging situations.

Our past experiences also teach us the importance of adaptability. Life is unpredictable, and we never know what the future holds. When we face unexpected situations, we have to adapt quickly; we have to make the needed changes in order to survive. This requires us to be flexible and open-minded. The more we practice adaptability, the better equipped we are to handle whatever the future throws our way. If we can learn from our past experiences and apply these lessons to the future, we will be better equipped to handle whatever situations we encounter.

CHAPTER 2

VALUE IN PERSEVERANCE

After several years of working in Jamaica in the hotel industry, I expanded my network to include individuals who loved what I did, and always encouraged me. I realized that there were more opportunities to study in London, and I eventually made the move to England. It was not an easy decision for me to leave the land of my birth, my family, friends, my beloved Ms. Dottie, and all that I knew in warm sunny Jamaica to start a new way of life in the cold United Kingdom, but I desired more growth and felt confident that could happen there.

However, despite the experience, and the certification I had garnered in Jamaica, it never mattered in England. Also, on account of some paperwork challenges as a new immigrant in the country, I had to literally start over my career.

Would you believe though, that just as how I started in Jamaica, I wasn't even initially allowed to cook?! Yes, that's right. Again, here I am assigned to washing pots, pans, and other dishes. I was not daunted, however, and I remained positive, and always did my best.

I remember at one of the places in which I worked, there was a manager there who was an English lady who had a warm, and kind personality. One day she observed how I was using the knife. Now this is what I mean when I say the experience I gained in Jamaica was preparation. Back home, I used to work on my knife skills in how I cut and prepare fruits, vegetables, you name it. She observed my skills and asked me about my expertise.

I seized the opportunity to explain to her that back in Jamaica I was working as a Chef and, as such, I had practiced and perfected my skills in using the knife. She and the other Executives had a discussion, and the decision was taken to upgrade my duties from washing the pots and dishes, to have me working in the kitchen as a Chef with about three other Chefs. Specifically, for me though, I would be preparing salads at the salad bar. In fact, I was assigned to the salad bar for an entire year! Nevertheless, I persevered. The saying is indeed correct that *your gift will make room for you.* I continued to do my best, even at the salad bar where I made an average of 18 scrumptious salads daily.

One of the early jobs that I also got in London was at an international residential private school working in the kitchen. This was what I called a 'posh' school, since it was attended by students from wealthy families. The meals prepared for the students and staff, understandably, were not the ordinary school lunch, but a rich, scrumptious cuisine daily. My duties included preparing three a la carte meals daily for the students and the staff. We also had to organize, and cater for functions such as graduations, children's parties, and Christmas dinners for the entire school community.

That role enabled me to start working at other private schools until I was placed as Head Chef at one of the schools. Can you believe that? Finally! After all these years before in Jamaica and in the UK washing dishes, pots, and pans, and learning from my superiors, I was finally placed in the top role. I truly learned the value of persistence.

Becoming Head Chef was really just the start. I worked even more diligently, and got the opportunity to showcase my passion, talent, and craft. As a result, I won several awards, got featured in the newspapers—the whole works. On one occasion in England, I was featured as one of nine national winners of an Outstanding Performance 2014 Award. During this time, I also obtained several certificates in the UK catering industry.

While still working as Head Chef at the school that I earlier mentioned, I also received another opportunity to also work as a Chef at another wealthy school. At this institution, I worked in the kitchen, and was res-ponsible for the preparation of meals for almost a thousand students, and staff combined daily. I embraced the opportunity since the work hours for me did not overlap. It was upon going to that institution that, as fate would have it, my journey into the lucrative, but more importantly fulfilling world of YouTube would begin.

Chef Ricardo after moving to London
and working as a Chef at a private
school.

Success Recipes from Chapter 2

My friend, perseverance is a valuable trait that can help you achieve your goals and overcome obstacles. Here are some of the proven benefits of perseverance for success.

1. *Achieving goals:* Perseverance helps you stay focused on your goals and take consistent action towards achieving them. It helps you overcome obstacles and setbacks that may arise along the way.

2. *Building resilience:* Perseverance helps you develop resilience, which is the ability to bounce back from adversity. It helps you develop a positive mindset and learn from failures.

3. *Developing self-discipline:* Perseverance requires self-discipline, which is the ability to control your impulses and stay focused on your goals. It helps you develop good habits and avoid distractions.

4. *Gaining confidence:* Perseverance helps you build confidence in yourself and your abilities. It shows you that you can overcome challenges and achieve your goals if you stay committed and focused.

5. *Inspiring others:* Perseverance can inspire others to pursue their own goals and dreams. When people see you persevering through challenges, they may be motivated to do the same.

Overall, perseverance is a valuable trait that can help you achieve success in all areas of your life. It requires commitment, resilience, and self-discipline, but the rewards are well worth the effort.

.

CHAPTER 3

YOU CAN LEARN FROM ANYONE

In this journey called life, I have learnt that you have to be willing to learn from anyone if you desire success in any capacity. You never know who could lead you down the path to your blessing. That was my situation.

Having started working in the kitchen at the second school, over time the students, and even the kitchen staff, would often be fascinated by my cooking skills. Sometimes it would simply be the way in which I cut the meat that would fascinate them. In a short space of time, my popularity had grown. After a brief period there, a young man joined the team. He worked part time in the kitchen washing pots and pans, similar to what I did when I was starting out my career. However, the interesting thing was that he drove a luxury car which would be almost impossible to buy for someone in that role as a dishwasher, earning that level salary.

One day, the young man said to me, *"Chef Ricardo, you should be a YouTuber."* He explained that he himself was a YouTuber and was making a good living from YouTube. However, he had become a little bored with that, and wanted something else to do in addition to that passion; hence the dishwasher role that he took on. The young man encouraged me to start a YouTube channel utilizing and displaying my skills as a Chef on the platform. He offered me some advice on how to get started on this new venture.

I was curious as to why he would have made the suggestion, and he told me how he and many others loved my style of cooking with my skills and flair. I had realized that, whenever I was preparing large quantities of meat to cut and season, the students, as well as my colleagues would love to record me and take photographs throughout the process of me blending my spices, marinating the meat, and more. They were also enamored with how I explained the processes in my Jamaican accent. I listened to the young man, took his advice, created the YouTube channel, and started from there. The channel was initially started as a hobby.

It's very important for me to say to you, though, that I was not an overnight success on YouTube. My journey to amassing millions of organic, and engaging subscribers, receiving the gold plaque from YouTube, and changing my financial fortunes, was no easy feat. However, it was overtime that my channel gained in popularity, and I started receiving positive feedback from viewers.

I initially knew nothing about YouTube, and in those early years, I didn't approach it seriously, and I wasn't consistent with posting. That young man had, however, continued to encourage me. Eventually, I got a videographer to help me to record the content, and I started being consistent on the platform. Later on, I started watching other YouTube videos to teach myself videography and editing for my content.

I eventually learned how to record and edit my own videos, as I wanted to always be able to put out content when I wanted, without having to wait for someone else to complete it. I continued to work hard on the YouTube channel, creating new recipes, and improving my video production skills. Taking it seriously, consistently posting my cooking videos without even really focusing on subscribers really helped.

I clearly remember the first time I earned fifty (50) US dollars from YouTube; I was pleasantly surprised, and that really encouraged me to continue. I told myself that this venture could be lucrative. Therefore, I proceeded to post even more content on YouTube, and to be even more consistent, as it proved to be a great avenue to showcase my skills, teach others to cook, and, as a bonus, earn, and boost my income.

In those early years, however, it was never about the money. My biggest motivation then was to get a YouTube play button; the plaque was the rave among all the YouTubers. You'll get a silver plaque when you reach one hundred thousand subscribers; gold when you reach a million subscribers; diamond when you reach ten million subscribers, and red diamond when you reach one hundred million subscribers. My goal was to get my first YouTube plaque.

I finally got my first silver plaque after amassing one hundred thousand subscribers, so my next target was the gold for reaching one million subscribers. With consistency, and determination I got it, and I was thrilled. The feeling of receiving that gold plaque from YouTube, to hold it in my hand, and then place it in my office, was just indescribable. Now, at the time of publication of this book, the diamond plaque for ten million subscribers is the next target.

What was a valuable lesson for me though was that upon introspection I wondered what If I had not taken that young man's advice, or dismissed it, because I thought he was too young. Even worse, what if I had let my own fears and doubts to embark on a journey I'd never attempted before stop me from taking that chance? My friend, I'm glad I listened. As you work towards being a success, never discount those who are teachers and instructors along the way even if they do not look how you expected. Take the chance and do it! Perhaps one day looking back like I'm doing; you'll be glad you did.

**Chef Ricardo's early years as a
YouTuber.**

Success Recipes from Chapter 3

Learning from anyone requires an open mind, curiosity, and a willingness to listen. Here are some success recipes on how to learn from anyone:

1. *Be curious:* Approach every interaction with curiosity and a desire to learn. Ask questions and listen to the other person's perspective.

2. *Be respectful:* Show respect for the other person's knowledge, experience, and perspective. Avoid judgment, or criticism, and be open to different ideas and opinions.

3. *Be attentive:* Pay attention to what the other person is saying and try to understand their point of view. Avoid distractions and give them your full attention.

4. *Be humble:* Recognize that you don't know everything and be open to learning from others. Don't be afraid to ask for help, or to admit when you don't know something.

5. *Be reflective:* After the interaction, take some time to reflect on what you learned and how it can be applied to improve your own life. Consider how

you can incorporate the new knowledge or perspective into your own thinking and behavior.

Remember, learning from anyone is a lifelong process that requires an open mind and a willingness to listen. By approaching every interaction with curiosity, and respect, you can learn from anyone and enrich your own life in the process.

CHAPTER 4
FAILURES ARE DETOURS, NOT A STOP SIGN

I don't often share this story but, on the road to success, believe it or not, failure is also an ingredient. You must be wondering if I'm crazy. How can failure be a recipe? Well listen, failure can be used as a launching pad, a motivation, or a tool to get you further along your desired end, or goal. While I was working at one of the wealthy private schools, I decided to start working on setting up my own business. In the autumn of 2010, I opened a small restaurant/takeaway called Chef Ricardo's Caribbean diner where I served up signature Caribbean dishes, and some with a unique twist. As the name suggested, it was all things Caribbean-related on the menu. The dishes were a hit among our customers.

Although this was an extremely difficult time due to the pressures of opening and establishing my own business, my customers and family gave me a lot of encouragement and support which made me very enthusiastic. It was also during this time that the idea came to me to produce my own sauces. I began to experiment, eventually inventing my own Caribbean sauce recipes such as 'Caribbean sunshine BBQ,' 'Caribbean jerk', 'brown stew', and 'curry jerk.' I worked hard at both the diner and the sauces. However, due to personal reasons, and family commitments, the restaurant ceased trading. It hurt; I'm human after all! However, it also put fuel to my fire to make a success story from the ashes of my failure.

The fuel was in pushing myself even more to become a success as a Chef on YouTube, so that this is not only a hobby but a viable livelihood where I can reach even more than just that diner but millions globally. It pushed me into writing my cookbook; to be part of several television productions globally showcasing my craft and to know that the road to success isn't always straight. Once you're passionate and love what you do, then my friend, myriads of opportunities will be there for you to shine and be your best self, as the Jamaican proverb goes "there's more than one way to skin a cat," which means there's more than one way of achieving one's goal.

Chef Ricardo in his
Caribbean diner in the UK
that he later closed.

Success Recipes from Chapter 4

Here are some success recipes on what I did and how you can do it:

1. *Learn from your mistakes.* Instead of dwelling on your failures, try to learn from them. Analyze what went wrong, and what you could have done differently. This will help you avoid making the same mistakes in the future.

2. *Stay positive.* It's easy to get discouraged after a failure, but it's important to stay positive. Focus on the lessons you've learned and the opportunities that lie ahead.

3. *Set new goals:* Use your failures as motivation to set new goals. This will help you stay focused and give you something to work toward.

4. *Take action:* Don't let your failures hold you back. Take action and keep moving forward. This will help you build momentum and achieve success.

5. *Embrace failure.* Failure is a natural part of the learning process. Embrace it and use it as an opportunity to grow and improve.

Remember my friend, success is not about avoiding failure, but about learning from it and using it to your advantage. With the right mindset and approach, you can turn your failures into success.

CHAPTER 5

THERE IS POWER IN YOUR WORDS

nything you need, and you speak it and mean it, it will happen. I shared those words with a TV Presenter and YouTuber from Jamaica on 'The Trailblazers with Tamara McKayle TV Show on YouTube' and, trust me; those words are so true. Your words have a life-force in them that is so powerful you can create your reality from the words you speak. To become a success in this life, watch how you speak. Watch how you talk about yourself as it very often manifests. Such was an experience for me in my earlier years in England.

The very first time I landed in the UK, I landed at the Gatwick airport in London. That same day, I said to myself out loud that I would love to work in that airport one day. I have never forgotten that day when I said those words to myself as I walked through the airport. Well, I'm going to tell you something; this in fact, happened in real life.

What happened was that at one point, I decided to move on from working in the chef role at schools, and I got a job with the ambulance services; perhaps I wanted a new challenge as well. During that time, I was still doing my YouTube show, but was able to garner new skillsets. I worked with the ambulance services for about one year then I started getting bored. Well, one day a friend said to me, *'Chef Ricardo why you don't come work where I am at Gatwick airport?'* Since I wanted to try something different, I agreed.

I went to Gatwick airport, which is the second largest airport in the UK, and filled out the job application form. I passed the relevant requirements and begun a job working around the aircrafts where we would get them ready for takeoff. I did this job for about a year. Do you now realize how potent your words are?

Remember when I had just arrived in England at the same airport commenting how I'd love to work there one day? Well talk about manifesting! There is indeed power in your words. You can indeed manifest your reality by what you say. A word of caution, however; the energy you have around you to get on your path to success is important, so be sure you have positive people in your circle who can encourage you, and who also speak positively. Most importantly, never forget to give thanks. It is through gratitude that we often open our blessings.

Success Recipes from Chapter 5

Here are some strategies on how to manifest your dreams using your words.

1. *Use positive language:* When manifesting, it's important to use positive language. Focus on what you want, rather than what you don't want. For example, instead of saying "I don't want to be broke," say "I am financially abundant." I have a friend who is very talented, and I know that she will make it big time. Every time I speak to her, I say, 'what's up Celebrity?' She has now begun to accept it in her mindset that this is part of who she is. Try this technique; it works!

2. *Be specific:* Be specific about what you want to see happen. The more specific you are, the easier it will be to visualize and attract what you desire.

3. *Use the present tense:* Use the present tense when manifesting. This helps to create the feeling that what you desire is already happening. For example, instead of saying "I will be successful," say "I am successful." Act as if it has already happened and your vibrational energy will attract it from doing so.

4. *Visualize:* Visualize yourself already having what you desire. This helps to create a clear picture in your mind and makes it easier for you to identify the manifestation.

5. *Believe:* I mentioned this word earlier when I said I had to believe what my grandma said that I would become a Chef one day. So, belief is key that what you desire is already on its way to you. Trust and have faith that your desires will manifest.

Remember manifesting using your words is a powerful tool, but it's important to take action towards your goals as well. Use your words to create a positive mindset and attract what you desire. Also take action toward making your dreams a reality.

CHAPTER 6
CONTINUOUSLY IMPROVE

A key recipe to my success to date is that I've always sought to improve myself, and to always be consistent. So often many of us reach a certain level of success, and then we become complacent, or comfortable. We stop doing all the things we did prior to reaching those heights. Never become stagnant or complacent in life.

Remember in Chapter 3 when I shared how my motivation when I started YouTube was to first get that play button, and the various plaques for achieving the targeted milestones? Well, while some may think it's a simple plaque, achieving those goals signaled to me that with consistency, perseverance, and passion, my dreams became possible. My quality of life, and standard of living, changed in that I no longer had to worry about money. YouTube changed my life a million percent, and that's a message I will gladly tell anyone. Do not watch the views, the subscribers, or anything; just keep posting. You never know what's going to happen. My friends, this is not just about YouTube; it is a testimony to remind you that your dreams, and goals are possible too.

It is through continuous improvement that I was able to finally step away from working for others to become my own boss. Although I was working for others, my quality of life from my earnings was not all that I had desired. If I hadn't improved myself, perhaps years later, I would have still been in the same position.

Deciding to improve myself, also pushed me some years ago to write my very first cookbook *'Chef Ricardo Caribbean Cuisine Cookbook',* featuring Caribbean recipes and dishes.

To this day, my success journey has been through consistency, dedication, and hard work. My YouTube family knows I'm in the kitchen cooking, and streaming, or uploading new videos every single day, sometimes several times a day. It's part of honouring myself, and being committed to my vision and, of course, to keep my community informed and engaged.

That's why I say to anyone no matter how young or old you are, you can do it! Whether it's to grow on YouTube, other social media platforms, or just about any dream, goal, or vision that you have.

An excited Chef Ricardo showing his YouTube gold plaque which he received after reaching his first million YouTube subscribers.

Success Recipes from Chapter 6

Here are some success recipes on how to continuously improve:

1. *Set goals:* Set specific, measurable, achievable, relevant, and time-bound (SMART) goals for yourself. This will help you stay focused and motivated.

2. *Learn new skills:* Continuously learn new skills and knowledge related to your field or interests. Attend workshops, read books, or listen to audio books, take online courses, or seek mentorship.

3. *Seek feedback:* Ask for constructive feedback from others, such as colleagues, friends, or family members. This will help you identify areas for improvement and make necessary changes. Be careful to filter the feedback as not everyone's opinion is the best for you. Try to get feedback from people you yourself admire and want to be like. If such a person is a celebrity for instance whom you may not necessarily know' then go to YouTube, and watch and learn from them!

4. *Reflect on your progress:* Take time to reflect on your progress and evaluate your performance. This will help you identify what's working, and

what's not working, and help you to make the necessary adjustments.

5. *Embrace challenges:* Embrace challenges and view them as opportunities for growth. Don't be afraid to step out of your comfort zone and to try new things.

6. *Practice self-care:* Take care of yourself physically, mentally, and emotionally. This will help you stay energized and focused on your goals. I'm big on this! I also prioritize what I eat. Of course, I have lots of videos on my YouTube Channel with healthy options to make you a better you.

Remember that continuous improvement is a journey, not a destination. It requires commitment, dedication, and a willingness to learn and grow. By following these tips, you can continuously improve and achieve your goals.

CHAPTER 7

A BALANCING ACT

The journey to the top requires balance. Balance and success are two important aspects of life that are often interconnected. Achieving balance in life means finding a healthy equilibrium between different areas of your life, such as work, family, relationships, hobbies, and personal growth. It involves prioritizing your time and energy to ensure that you are not neglecting any important aspect of your life.

While I was working as a Chef at that private school, my beautiful daughter Kayla was born, and the truth is that was even more motivation for me to be successful. I note, however, that success is multifaceted. Therefore, as someone who works hard, is very focused, and driven, I have to be intentional about daddy/daughter time. For instance, I would work, do my YouTube show, and then also find time for us to hang out. Hanging out could be simple tasks such as picking her up from school, or other activities like going on a playdate.

None of us is perfect. However, in order to achieve balance and success, there needs to be a combination of self-awareness, goal-setting, and consistent effort. It is important to identify your priorities and values, set realistic goals, and take consistent action toward achieving them. It is also important to take care of your physical and mental health, maintain positive relationships, and cultivate a sense of purpose, and meaning in your life. Nothing is wrong with being happy.

Ultimately, finding balance and success is a personal journey that requires self-reflection, perseverance, and a willingness to learn, and grow.

Creating balance in your life is essential for your overall well-being. It is important to find a balance between work, family, friends, hobbies, and personal time. When you have balance in your life, you are able to manage stress better, have more energy, and feel more fulfilled.

Chef Ricardo and his
beautiful daughter Kayla
several years ago.

Success Recipes from Chapter 7

Here are some important recipes on how to execute the balancing act.

1. *Prioritize*: One way to create balance in your life is to prioritize your time. Make a list of the things that are most important to you and allocate time for each of them. This will help you to avoid feeling overwhelmed and will ensure that you are giving attention to the things that matter most.

2. *Learn to say no*: Another way to create balance is to learn to say no at times. It is important to set boundaries, and not take on too much. Saying no can be difficult, but it is necessary to avoid burnout and maintain balance in your life.

3. *Self-care*: Taking care of your physical health is also important for creating balance. Make sure to get enough sleep, exercise regularly, and maintain a healthy diet. When you feel good physically, it is easier to manage stress, and maintain balance in your life.

4. *Finally, make time for yourself.* Whether it is reading a book, taking a bath, or going for a walk, it is important to have time to recharge and do things that make you happy.

Creating balance in your life is essential for your overall well-being. By prioritizing your time, setting boundaries, taking care of your physical health, and making time for yourself, you can achieve balance and live a happier, more fulfilling life.

CHAPTER 8

FOCUS

Having left Jamaica as a poor youngster, and later becoming the successful man I am now in the UK was no easy feat. My aim is not to brag or boast, but to simply share with others that it can be done. So often we think it can't be done, but it can. You just have to FOCUS!

Forget the limitations that have been set by society, or even those around you. I love the fact that while I'm pursuing my passion, which is cooking, using a platform such as YouTube has allowed me to connect with people from various nations. What are you waiting on to get started on your own journey? Whether it's starting a YouTube channel, or some other goal, start NOW. Start, even if you feel like you don't have all the things you think you need to. Begin where you are. If you love something and you do it from your heart, then my friend, success will follow.

If you keep the vision of your dreams or goals in mind, and you really work hard at it while using some of the other secret success recipes that I mentioned, you can achieve your goals.

Success Recipes from Chapter 8

Here are some tips to help you focus:

1. *Eliminate distractions:* Try to remove any distractions that may be hindering your focus. This could include turning off your phone, closing unnecessary tabs on your computer, or finding a quiet place in which to work.

2. *Set goals:* Having clear goals in mind can help you stay focused on what you need to accomplish. Write down your goals and prioritize them to help you stay on track.

3. *Take breaks.* Taking short breaks can actually help you stay focused in the long run. Try taking a 5 to 10-minute break every hour or so, to give your brain a chance to rest and recharge.

4. *Use a timer:* Set a timer for a specific amount of time, and work on a task until the timer goes off. This can help you stay focused and avoid getting distracted.

5. *Practice mindfulness.* Mindfulness is the practice of being present in the moment and focusing on your thoughts and feelings. Try practicing mindfulness exercises to help improve your focus and concentration.

Remember, focusing takes practice and patience. Don't get discouraged if you find yourself getting distracted - just take a deep breath and try again.

My friends remember this, don't give up! Keep the faith. Pray. Work towards your goal and your dream and it will happen in real life. Share your passion and get up out of your comfort zone!

CHAPTER 9

PRACTICE GRATITUDE

I It may seem simple, but one of my secret recipes to success is simply being grateful. Gratitude helps to cultivate a positive mindset, which is essential for success. When you are grateful for what you have, you are more likely to focus on the positive aspects of your life, and to be optimistic about the future.

Most of the opportunities I've attracted/received were just from simply being grateful. I remember recently travelling to the Dominican Republic for a television production and, just being grateful for that opportunity led to connections and opportunities with other like-minded and successful Chefs who are global trailblazers and influencers.

Success Recipes from Chapter 9

Here are some tips to practice being more grateful.

1. *Keep a gratitude journal:* Write down three things you are grateful for each day. This can help you focus on the positive things in your life.

2. *Express gratitude to others:* Take the time to thank someone who has helped you or made a positive impact on your life. This can be done in person, through a phone call, or even a handwritten note.

3. *Focus on the present moment:* Take a few minutes each day to focus on the present moment and appreciate what you have in your life right now.

4. *Practice mindfulness:* Mindfulness meditation can help you become more aware of your thoughts and feelings and can help you cultivate a sense of gratitude.

5. *Use positive affirmations.* Repeat positive affirmations to yourself each day, such as "I am grateful for all the good things in my life" or "I am thankful for the people who love and support me."

Remember, practicing gratitude is a habit that takes time and effort to develop. But with consistent practice, you can cultivate a more positive and grateful mindset.

CHAPTER 10

USING YOUTUBE TO YOUR ADVANTAGE

Growing a YouTube channel past 1.5 million subscribers is no easy feat and I know the journey to not only start but also continue has its ups and downs. This is why I wanted to share some practical strategies in this chapter that you can begin to use today to elevate your YouTube channel and take it to the next level. I encourage you to start no matter your skillset, education, background, you name it. It doesn't matter. Once you have an area you're passionate about, or in which you have an interest, you can join the

YouTube community. It's free and, yes; it will take some work to build yourself. However, think of the long-term benefits. Although I'm the first Jamaican Chef to get a YouTube Gold plaque for surpassing a million subscribers, there are millions of YouTubers around the world in various fields and industries; various age groups, weight, height, skin colour, you name it that have completely revolutionized their lives by becoming their own bosses through YouTube and working successfully, even living a life of luxury. You can do it too!

Success Recipes from Chapter 10

Here are some other success recipes to use to grow your YouTube channel.

1. *Don't think it has to be something fancy or extravagant.* I like cooking, so I cook, and showcase my craft on YouTube. For you, it could be gaming, climbing a tree, or showcasing where you live, there are so many ideas you may explore, and attempt. Just generally try to select ideas around areas that you love so it makes it easier for you to do.

2. *Focus on your idea/ideas.* The word focus will continue to recur because consistency is key to

helping you get to the next level. I know I love the word consistency, but it's important to have that 'stick-to-itiveness' to reach your dream or goal. Consistency is key when it comes to growing a YouTube channel. You should upload videos on a regular basis if you're serious about growing the channel. Whether it's several times a week, or once a week, a regular schedule helps. This will also help your viewers to know when to expect new content from you.

3. *Use what you have to start.* Yes, quality is key and we want good content that we can at least see clearly and hear well. However, you don't have to go out and get some fancy expensive camera or equipment to start. Just start. Many YouTubers are simply using their phone and still raking in large amounts of money monthly. It just depends on how you use it. Later on when you have grown and acquired some decent earnings, if you feel led to, then you can consider getting a fancy camera. To start, however, simply use what you have, right where you are. You never know, you could be among the big leagues on YouTube!

4. *Define your area of focus, or as some of us call it, your niche.* This simply means you have specific areas on which your YouTube channel focuses.

My channel is a cooking/food channel; yours could be sports, entertainment, news updates, and interviews, fashion; the topics are wide and varied. While no one is limiting you, it's ideal to start off to focus and zoom in on a specific area so your new audience will come to know what to expect from the type of content that you are putting out. You can, in fact, have your channel focus on multiple topics, but again, it's good to define it from the get-go. You can also have multiple channels. However, as a start, I'd suggest that you focus on one channel at a time and expand it while you're building your audience.

5. *Make your channel a part of your brand.* This is extremely important, especially in a world that is heavily influenced by social media. We are all a brand; believe it or not. Don't think it's only the Hollywood stars or the popular YouTubers, or social media influencers that are brands. You are your own billboard by the way you carry yourself, and the very content that you create. People, or let's use the word viewers or subscribers, gain insights about who you are from the content you create. Therefore, ensure that it's a brand that represents what you intentionally want to put out there. From doing this and focusing on your

niche/niches, you can also gain lucrative brand-deals, sponsors and grow even more.

6. Learn from YouTube. Many of us see YouTube as a University. On the platform, you can learn just about anything. A great way to grow in your niche is simply to research a topic of interest on YouTube and learn from other content creators on how to grow your channel; how to grow in your niche. You name it. Learning information such as: Search Engine Optimization (SEO), which is important for YouTube channels. Also, how to use relevant keywords in your video titles, descriptions, and tags to help your videos rank higher in search results. These can all be learned on the YouTube platform.

My Charge to You

Although growing up in Jamaica was a pleasant experience, it was economically challenging. However, I kept focused, and avoided being led astray. That's the main thing you'll have to do. Focus! Yes, it is important for you to keep focused. Tell yourself, this is what you want. I will tell anyone in this world. Anyone. If you need something in this world, trust me, you can get it. You have to just focus and work towards your goal.

I thank you for your support as I continue to cook and create, always pushing the boundaries, and exploring new flavors and techniques. I will always remain a true ambassador for Jamaican cuisine. Thank you. In the next several pages, enjoy the free recipes of mouthwatering goodness. Some were inspired by my Grandma Ms. Dottie so I'm just passing on the love.

CHAPTER 11

SOME OF CHEF RICARDO'S FAVOURITE RECIPES

Sweet Potato Pudding

Ingredients

- 2 cups plain flour
- ¾ cups cornmeal
- 1 tsp. cinnamon powder
- 1 tsp Jamaican nutmeg
- 1 tsp. mixed spice
- 1 tsp. baking powder
- A pinch of salt
- 2 lb. sweet potato, peeled and grated
- A pinch of coconut, grated
- 8 oz. yam, grated
- 1 tsp. butter
- 1 tbsp. vanilla essence
- 2 cups liquid coconut milk
- 1 tsp. molasses
- 1 cup. brown sugar

For the sauce:
- 4 oz. coconut milk
- 2 tbsp. brown sugar
- 1 tsp. vanilla

Method

- Preheat your oven. Grease your baking tray and set aside.

- Sieve the flour, cornmeal, cinnamon powder, nutmeg, mixed spice, baking powder and salt.

- Set aside.

- In a separate bowl, add the grated potato, coconut, yam, butter and the liquid ingredients in.

- Stir to combine.

- Add coconut milk. Add molasses and sugar. Stir.

- Add the dry ingredients, one cup at a time, to the moist ingredients and cut and fold.

- Transfer the batter to the greased baking pan.

- Place the baking pan in a tray with water. Cover with aluminum foil.

- Bake for 1 hour.

- Remove from the oven. Set aside.

For the sauce:

- In a measuring cup, pour in the coconut milk and sugar. Stir.

- Add vanilla and stir once more.
- Pour on top of the pudding.
- Let it bake for 15 minutes more.
- Remove from oven and set aside to cool.
- Serve.

Preparation Time: 1 hour 46 minutes

Serving Size: Family size

Chef Tips: Avoid getting the yellow skin sweet potato. The red skinned potato is best. It's okay if it starts to change color when grating. Raisins can be added.

Benefits of Sweet Potatoes:

- It is a great source of fiber, vitamins, and minerals.

- The fibers in sweet potatoes are advantageous to gut health.

- It enhances brain functioning.
- It supports your immune system.

- It helps to reduce the risk of cancer.

- It helps to manage type-2 diabetes.

- They also help to support your vision.

Jamaican Pumpkin Punch

Ingredients

- 1/4 lb. pumpkin, peeled, cut into small pieces
- 2 cups water
- A pinch of nutmeg
- A pinch of cinnamon powder
- A pinch of mixed spice
- 1 tsp. molasses
- 1 tsp Jamaican vanilla
- 3tsp Jamaican sweetened condensed milk
- 1/2 can Irish mash
- Supligen (vanilla)
- 1/2 can Jamaican nutriment
- 1/2 can Jamaican Guinness punch
- Ice (optional)

Method:

- Wash the pumpkin pieces properly. Put washed pumpkin into a pot and add the cups of water.

- Leave it to boil for 10 minutes. After it is boiled, drain the water, and leave it to cool until it has reached room temperature. Once cooled, put it in the blender. Add other ingredients to the blender. Cover and blend for 45 seconds – 1 minute.

- Serve with ice (optional) and enjoy.

Preparation Time: 30 minutes

Serving Size: up to two persons

Chef Tips: Adding too much cinnamon powder to the drink might give it an "off" taste. Fresh pumpkin is ideal for this drink.

Healthy Stir-fry Cabbage

Ingredients

- 1 tsp. olive oil
- 1/2 cabbage, finely chopped
- 2 cloves garlic, chopped
- 2 medium size carrots, chopped
- 1 tomato, chopped
- Mixed peppers
- 4 stalks spring onion
- 1 white onion, finely chopped
- A pinch of coast pepper
- A pinch of salt
- A pinch of all-purpose seasoning
- A pinch of mixed herbs

Method:

- Pour olive oil into your frying pan and add the garlic, cabbage, mixed peppers, spring onions, white onion, and carrot into the frying pan.

- Put the frying pan on the stove on medium heat, add powdered ingredients; and add salt to the vegetables. Fry for 10-15 minutes while stirring.

- Remove from the heat and serve.

Preparation Time: 25 minutes

Serving Size: up to 3 persons

Chef Tips: Ensure to get rid of the stem of the cabbage before preparing, it is not needed. Can be served with rice.

Pineapple Upside Down Cake

Ingredients

- 1 cup honey or sugar
- Pineapple slices
- Cherries
- 8 oz. unsalted butter
- 8 oz. sugar
- 4 eggs, beaten
- 8 oz. self-raising flour, sieved
- 1 tsp. cinnamon
- A pinch of baking powder
- 1 tsp. vanilla extract
- 1/4 cup milk
- 1 tsp. pineapple flavouring

Method

- Grease your 256 cm baking pan with honey, give it 3 minutes in the oven, gas marked 3.

- Line it with pineapple slices and cherries and set aside.

- In a separate bowl, blend together the butter and sugar, using the creaming method. Hand mixers can be used.

- Sieve the flour along with cinnamon and baking powder together.

. Add the egg to the batter, one at a time, and cut and fold while adding the vanilla, pineapple flavouring, and milk to the batter until the batter is thoroughly mixed. Beat for 1 minute with a hand mixer.

- Transfer the pineapple cake mixture on top of the honey and pineapple slices.

- Bake for 1/2 hour.
- Remove from the oven. Flip it upside down for perfect results.
- Serve.

***Preparation Time*:** up to 1 hour

Serving Size: 12 persons

Chef Tips: Brown sugar can be used also to line the baking pan.

Christmas Black Rum
Fruit Cake

Ingredients

- 500 g. raisins
- 2 cups red label wine
- 1 tsp. Wray and nephew wine
- 1 cup red berries
- 12 oz. unsalted butter
- 8 oz. brown sugar
- 12 oz. plain flour, sieved
- 2 tsp. baking powder, sieved
- 1 tsp. mixed spice, sieved
- 1 tsp. nutmeg, sieved
- A pinch of cinnamon, sieved
- A pinch of salt
- 4 medium sized eggs
- 1 lemon, grated
- 3 1/2 tsp browning

Method

- Preheat your oven (gas marked 6 or 7 /150 degrees), grease your baking pan with the butter and 1 tsp. of plain flour.

- Blend together the raisins with the red label wine, Wray and nephew together.

- Remove it from the blender and blend the berries in 1/2 cup of wine. Pour it out on top of the raisins.

- Fold the butter and sugar together until it's creamed.

- Combine the flour and spices together, then add it to the butter mixture with salt.

- Add the eggs, one at a time, and whisk.

- Add the grated lemon and whisk.

- Add the fruits, 1 cup at a time, and the flour, one cup at a time, and cut and fold.

- Add browning to enhance the color.

- Transfer the batter into the baking pan and let it bake for 45 minutes.

- Remove it from the oven, brush with rum and wine.

- Serve and enjoy.

Preparation Time: up to 1 hour

Serving Size: up to 10 persons

Chef Tips: The raisins should not be too fine when they are blended. Mixed fruits can be used. Lemons bring the best flavors to the cake. Too much browning will make the cake too black, or even bitter. Use only up to 4 tsps. of browning if the color is not desired.

Easy Banana and Coconut
Cake

Ingredients

- 4 oz. unsalted butter, melted
- 1 tsp. grated coconut
- 4 oz. self raising flour, sieved
- 2 medium sized eggs
- 4 oz. granulated sugar
- 1 baking tray
- 1 finger ripe banana, sliced
- 1 tsp. vanilla
- A pinch of baking powder
- A pinch of salt

Method

- Preheat your oven at 165 degrees (5 1/2 pr 6 1/2 in gas marked). Grease your baking tray with spray oil or butter and flour the pan. Lay a few banana slices in the baking pan and set aside, covered.
- Pour the butter into a large bowl. Add the sugar and whisk together.
- Add the vanilla and whisk.
- Add the eggs, one at a time, and beat them in.
- Add the flour, salt, and baking powder (1 cup at a time) to the batter. Cut and fold in the process.

- Add the grated coconut to the cake batter and stir to combine.
- Pour the mixture half way on top of the banana pieces in the baking pan, add a few more of the banana slices to the batter then add the rest of the batter in the baking pan. Add the remaining banana pieces to the top of the batter and sprinkle with the remaining grated coconut.
- Bake for 30- 35 minutes.
- Remove it from the oven. Let it cool and serve.

Preparation Time: up to 1 hour

Serving Size: 6 persons

Chef Tips: Tap the baking tin with the batter in it to avoid air to be in the cake once it is baked.

Banana Bread

Ingredients

- 4 oz. unsalted butter, melted
- 8 oz. coaster sugar
- 2 room temp. Eggs
- 1 1/2 tsp. lemon juice
- 3 fingers ripe bananas, crushed
- 2 tsp. vanilla essence
- 8 oz flour, sieved
- 2 tsp. baking soda, sieved
- 1/2 tsp. salt
- 8 oz. milk

Method

- Preheat your oven at gas marked 4 and grease your baking pan.
- Whisk together the butter and sugar.
- Add the eggs and lemon juice. Whisk together.
- Add the bananas to the batter. Whisk it in.
- Add the vanilla extract and cut and fold it in.
- Add the dry ingredients, 1 cup at a time and beat with a hand mixer.
- Add the milk, and cut and fold it in, little by little.

- Pour the bread batter into the baking pan and bake it for 30 minutes.
- Remove it from the oven and let it cool, then serve.

Preparation Time: up to 1 hour.

Serving Size: 4- 5 persons

Chef Tips: You can use a hand mixer in the preparing process. You can add fruits and raisins to the batter for better results.

One of the Jamaicans' Top
Ten BBQ Chicken Recipes

Ingredients

- 1 lb. chicken, washed, cleaned, and chopped
- 1 medium sized red onion, chopped
- 3 stalks spring onion, diced
- Thyme
- Ginger, finely chopped
- A pinch of soy sauce
- 1 tsp. paprika
- 1 tsp. all-purpose seasoning
- 1 tsp. BBQ seasoning
- 1 tsp. chicken seasoning
- A pinch of BBQ sauce
- 1 tsp. olive oil
- Oven tray

For the Sauce:

- BBQ sauce
- Honey

Method

- Preheat your oven. Line the oven tray with grease paper and set aside.

- Add the natural seasonings, soy sauce, paprika, all-purpose seasoning, BBQ seasoning, chicken seasoning, BBQ sauce, and olive oil to the chicken. Rub together, then gently place each piece of chicken on the grease paper.

- Bake for 35 minutes. Remove it from the heat, then dip each piece into the BBQ sauce, after which you put them on a clean greased sheet, then have it bake for another 10 minutes.

- Remove it from the heat then serve.

Preparation Time: up to 1 hour

Serving Size: up to 3 persons

Chef Tips: This can be served with rice and peas or bread.

French Fried Chicken

Ingredients

- 1 whole white onion, peeled, cut into quarters
- 1 head garlic, cleaned
- 1 kg. chicken, skinless, washed
- 2 tbsp. everyday seasoning
- 1 tsp. paprika
- A pinch of pepper
- 1 tsp. garlic and chilli spices
- 1 tsp. dried pimento seeds
- 1 tsp. mixed spice
- 1 tsp. hot pepper sauce
- 1 tsp. mixed herbs
- 1 cup cooking oil
- 1 tsp. olive oil

For the Flour:

- 1 tsp. everyday seasoning
- 1 cup cooking flour
- 1 tsp. paprika
- A pinch of pepper
- 1/2 tsp. dried chilli
- 1 tsp. dried herbs

For the Egg Wash:

- 1 cup cooking flour
- 6 eggs
- 1 tsp. everyday seasoning
- 1 tsp. dried paprika
- 1 tsp. sugar
- 1 tsp. chilli sauce
- 1 tsp. hot pepper sauce

Method

- Season the flour with paprika, pepper, chilli, herbs, and everyday seasoning, then stir.

- Season the chicken with everyday seasoning, paprika, pepper, garlic and chilli, dried pimento seeds, mixed spice, hot pepper sauce, and mixed herbs. Rub the seasonings on the chicken. This can be covered and used on the next day.

- For the egg wash, pour milk into a large bowl, then add eggs. Add seasonings to the egg wash and whisk.

- Heat skillet then add oil.

- Once the oil is heated, add the onion and cloves of garlic to enhance the oil's flavour.

- Meanwhile, dip pieces of chicken one at at a time into the egg wash, then flour it (shake off excessive flour to avoid a mess from the counter to the pot), after which you put it into the frying pan. After the first batch is in, turn down the flame to avoid burns. Have it fried for 10- 15 minutes. Repeat the process until each piece of chicken is fried.

- Serve with rice and enjoy.

Preparation Time: 1 hour

Serving Size: 4-5 persons

Chef Tips: You can add pepper to the oil so the chicken can have a spicy flavor. You can add egg wash to the seasoned chicken for faster results. You can also add onions to the oil for amazing results.

About the Author

Chef Ricardo is a Jamaican author, award-winning Chef and Gold plaque YouTuber with over 1.5 million subscribers on his main YouTube channel. With over 20 years of experience in the kitchen at various levels, Chef Ricardo has successfully taken his love for food and the kitchen to a global audience through his digital platforms.

Chef Ricardo now lives in the United Kingdom, where he continues to use his palate and voice to inspire and encourage others. He believes that through passion, hard work and consistency, all your dreams can be achieved. You can find Chef Ricardo on YouTube at youtube.com/@ChefRicardoCooking.

BOOK REVIEWS

If you enjoyed this book and were impacted by it, tell a friend, and please write an honest review wherever you bought it online. Book reviews are the lifeblood of authors. It is social proof.